Date: 3/12/14

Road Trip: Exploring America's Regions

Let's Explore the

MIDWEST

BY KATHLEEN CONNORS

Gareth Stevens
Publishing

Please visit our website, www.garethstevens.com. For a free color catalog of all our high-quality books, call toll free 1-800-542-2595 or fax 1-877-542-2596.

Library of Congress Cataloging-in-Publication Data

Connors, Kathleen.
 Let's explore the Midwest / Kathleen Connors.
     pages cm. — (Road trip: exploring America's regions)
 Includes index.
 ISBN 978-1-4339-9130-1 (pbk.)
 ISBN 978-1-4339-9131-8 (6-pack)
 ISBN 978-1-4339-9129-5 (library binding)
 1. Middle West—Juvenile literature. I. Title. II. Title: Let us explore the Midwest.
 F351.C6925 2013
 917.704'34—dc23

                                         2012049130

First Edition

Published in 2014 by
Gareth Stevens Publishing
111 East 14th Street, Suite 349
New York, NY 10003

Copyright © 2014 Gareth Stevens Publishing

Designer: Andrea Davison-Bartolotta
Editor: Kristen Rajczak

Photo credits: Cover, p. 1 (left) Nancy Gill/Shutterstock.com, (right) iStockphoto/Thinkstock; cover, backcover, interior backgrounds (texture) Marilyn Volan/Shutterstock.com; cover, backcover (map) Stacey Lynne Payne/ Shutterstock.com; cover, backcover, pp. 1, 22–24 (green sign) Shutterstock.com; interior backgrounds (road) Renata Novackova/Shutterstock.com, (blue sign) Vitezslav Valka/Shutterstock.com; pp. 4, 5 (map), 9 (state outline), 18 iStockphoto/Thinkstock; p. 5 (curled corner) JonnyDrake/Shutterstock.com, (background) Brand X Pictures/Thinkstock; p. 7 Stockbyte/Thinkstock; p. 9 (background map) AridOcean/Shutterstock.com; p. 10 Martin Hass/Shutterstock.com; p. 11 Jodi Baglien Sparkes/Shutterstock.com; p. 12 Kenny Tong/Shutterstock.com; p. 13 Ffooter/Shutterstock.com; p. 15 Raymond Boyd/Michael Ochs Archives/Getty Images; p. 17 courtesy of National Parks Service via Wikimedia Commons; p. 19 (both) courtesy of Wikimedia Commons; p. 20 LCDM Universal History Archive/Getty Images.

Printed in the United States of America

CPSIA compliance information: Batch #CS13GS: For further information contact Gareth Stevens, New York, New York at 1-800-542-2595.

Contents

Words in the glossary appear in **bold** type the first time they are used in the text.

The Heart of a Nation

Often called the "heartland," the Midwest **region** of the United States is a big part of our nation. It's located in the northern center of the country. The map below highlights the Midwest and the 12 states the US Census Bureau includes in it.

With all those states to travel through, no road trip across America could be complete without a few stops in the Midwest! It has something for every traveler, from a building covered in corn and cornhusks to historic Mount Rushmore.

The Midwest

The Midwest is made up of big cities, small farming communities, and everything in between. Its total population is almost 67 million!

The Midwest
at a Glance

	State	Population (2010)	Date of Statehood	Capital	State Bird	State Flower
1	**Illinois**	12,830,632	Dec. 3, 1818	Springfield	northern cardinal	violet
2	**Indiana**	6,483,802	Dec. 11, 1816	Indianapolis	northern cardinal	peony
3	**Iowa**	3,046,355	Dec. 28, 1846	Des Moines	eastern goldfinch	wild prairie rose
4	**Kansas**	2,853,118	Jan. 29, 1861	Topeka	western meadowlark	common sunflower
5	**Michigan**	9,883,640	Jan. 26, 1837	Lansing	American robin	apple blossom and dwarf lake iris
6	**Minnesota**	5,303,925	May 11, 1858	St. Paul	common loon	pink and white lady's slipper
7	**Missouri**	5,988,927	Aug. 10, 1821	Jefferson City	eastern bluebird	hawthorn blossom
8	**Nebraska**	1,826,341	March 1, 1867	Lincoln	western meadowlark	giant goldenrod
9	**North Dakota**	672,591	Nov. 2, 1889	Bismark	western meadowlark	wild prairie rose
10	**Ohio**	11,536,504	March 1, 1803	Columbus	northern cardinal	scarlet carnation and white trillium
11	**South Dakota**	814,180	Nov. 2, 1889	Pierre	ring-necked pheasant	American pasqueflower
12	**Wisconsin**	5,686,986	May 29, 1848	Madison	American robin	wood violet

Great Plains, Badlands

The area called the Midwest today was added to the United States in two parts. The **Northwest Territory** became part of the country in the 1780s. The Great Plains were added as part of the **Louisiana Purchase** in 1803. The Great Plains are a huge area of grasslands covering much of Kansas, Nebraska, North Dakota, and South Dakota.

Unlike the Great Plains, the Midwest's Badlands grow very few plants! Located in South Dakota, the Badlands have great **mesas** and jagged, rocky hills.

Pit Stop

The second-longest river in the United States, the Missouri River, flows through the Great Plains. Sioux City, Iowa, and Kansas City, Missouri, are cities along the Missouri.

You can visit the Badlands! About 380 square miles (984 sq km) of this cool geographic wonder became a national park in 1978.

Waterways

No tour of the Midwest would be complete without a fishing trip. That's because the Midwest is home to both the upper part of the Mississippi River and four of the Great Lakes!

The Mississippi River serves as a natural border for Wisconsin, Iowa, Illinois, Missouri, and part of Minnesota. There's no shortage of museums and other historic sites in these states along the river. Fort Snelling, a US military fort built in the 1820s, is located where the Mississippi meets the Minnesota River.

Pit Stop

The Mississippi River starts at Lake Itasca in Park Rapids, Minnesota. At Itasca State Park, the river is so narrow that visitors can walk across it!

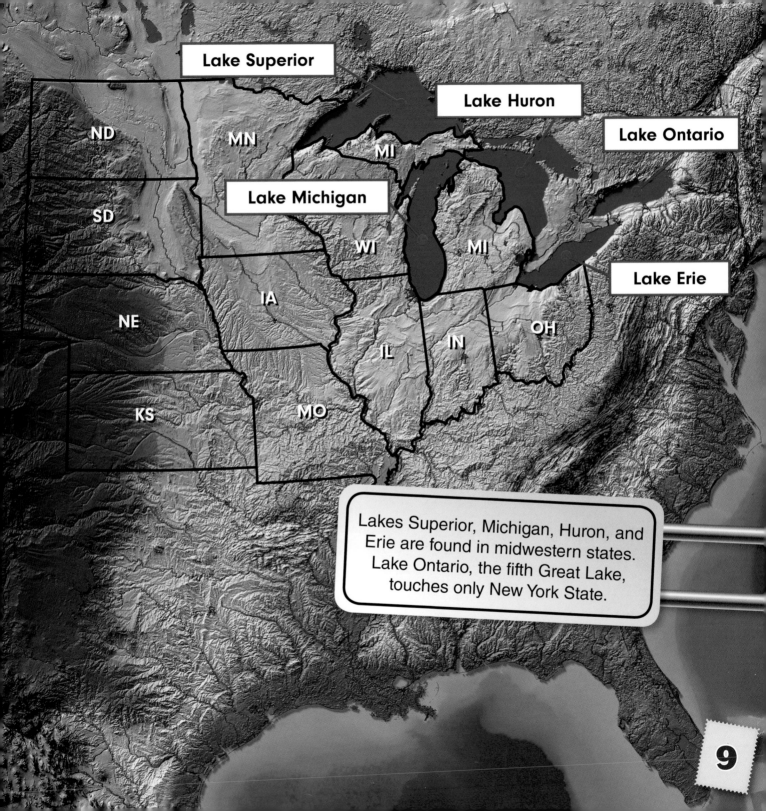

Lake Superior

Lake Huron

Lake Ontario

ND

MN

MI

Lake Michigan

SD

WI

MI

NE

IA

Lake Erie

IL

IN

OH

KS

MO

Lakes Superior, Michigan, Huron, and Erie are found in midwestern states. Lake Ontario, the fifth Great Lake, touches only New York State.

Weather the Weather

Taking a road trip through the Midwest can be a packing challenge—especially if you're planning on staying awhile. The **climate** includes all four seasons. There can be a 100-degree difference in temperature between summer and winter! However, because of the size of the Midwest, much of the weather depends on where you live.

In Duluth, Minnesota, about 80 inches (203 cm) of snow falls each year. Wichita, Kansas, on the other hand, has only about 15 inches (38 cm) of annual snowfall.

St. Peters, Missouri, after a heavy snow

A road trip through the Midwest during the winter could be dangerous. When it snows, roads can be slippery and hard to drive on.

Pit Stop

Being both in the middle of North America and near the Great Lakes causes the great shifts in weather from season to season in the Midwest.

Big City Living

Traveling through the Midwest by car, you might take Interstate 90. This highway connects many of the region's cities, including Cleveland, Ohio; Gary, Indiana; and Chicago, Illinois.

Chicago is the third-largest city in the United States, with a population of about 2.7 million. It was the second-largest city in the country in 1890, only about 60 years after being founded! Today, Chicago has ballet companies, sports teams, and a famous silver sculpture in one of its parks. Visitors often call it "the bean"!

Pit Stop

Another well-known midwestern city, St. Louis, Missouri, is home to the Gateway **Arch**. This stunning arch, which is 630 feet (192 m) tall, was built to honor St. Louis as the "gateway to the West."

The silver, bean-shaped piece of art in Chicago's Millennium Park is actually called "Cloud Gate." Millennium Park is home to many other modern art pieces, too.

13

Famous Faces

From the Wright brothers to Walt Disney, many famous Americans have hailed from the Midwest. Some of them have historic sites and museums you can visit.

At the Mark Twain Boyhood Home and Museum in Hannibal, Missouri, visitors can learn all about the man who wrote *Tom Sawyer* right where he was born. In Atchison, Kansas, the Amelia Earhart Birthplace Museum gives a glimpse into the life of the famous female pilot before she disappeared on a round-the-world flight in 1937.

Pit Stop

Robert Wadlow, the tallest man in history, was from Alton, Illinois. His hometown put up a life-size statue of him in 1985. Like Wadlow, the statue stands 8 feet 11 inches (272 cm) tall!

Several presidents have called the Midwest home, including Abraham Lincoln (Illinois) and Harry Truman (Missouri), among others.

15

The Earliest Settlers

Before any settlers set foot in North America, ancient Native American tribes lived in the Midwest. In fact, mounds of earth built by them date back thousands of years! The Effigy Mounds National Monument allows visitors a close look while learning about Native American history.

Today, more than 30 tribes live in Michigan, Wisconsin, Minnesota, Illinois, Indiana, and Ohio. Some may be **descendants** of Native Americans who fought the US government in the 1800s. They wanted to stay on land they had occupied for generations.

Pit Stop

Native American leader Sitting Bull fought to keep **sacred** land in the Black Hills of South Dakota. Though the monument to the famous Battle of the Little Bighorn is in Montana, Sitting Bull's remains rest in Mobridge, South Dakota.

Effigy Mounds National Monument is in Harpers Ferry, Iowa.

17

Farm and Food

The Great Plains of the Midwest are beautiful to visit. They are also some of the most productive farmland in the United States. Corn, cattle, and soybeans, three of the top **exports** in the country, are all produced in great amounts in the Midwest. About half of the United States' exported wheat is grown there, too.

Travelers through the Midwest won't forget that it's called the nation's "breadbasket." The region is known for hearty comfort foods, often made with grains grown right on the Great Plains.

Cincinnati Chili

Ingredients:

1 quart cold water
2 lbs ground beef
2 cups crushed tomatoes
2 yellow onions, diced
4 garlic cloves, chopped
1 tbsp Worcestershire sauce
1 tbsp unsweetened cocoa
1/4 cup chili powder
1 tsp cayenne
1 tsp ground cumin
2 tbsp cider vinegar
1 whole bay leaf
1/4 tsp ground cloves
1 tsp cinnamon
1 1/2 tsp salt

Directions:

1. Add water and beef to a big pot. Simmer while mixing it until the beef is in very small pieces, about 30 minutes.

2. Add the rest of the ingredients.

3. Simmer on low heat for 3 hours. If the chili starts to thicken, add water as needed.

4. Serve over cooked spaghetti or top with cheese, onions, beans, or a combination of these!

You may have heard of deep-dish pizza in Chicago and barbeque in Kansas City, Missouri. But did you know Cincinnati, Ohio, has a famous **chili**? Ask an adult to help you follow these directions to make this yummy dish. It's sometimes served over spaghetti!

Mount Rushmore

Gold, silver, and copper have all been found in the Black Hills of South Dakota. These mountains are also home to a huge herd of bison. But the most famous part of the Black Hills is man-made.

The faces of George Washington, Thomas Jefferson, Abraham Lincoln, and Theodore Roosevelt were carved into Mount Rushmore from 1927 to 1941. Today, more than 3 million people visit Mount Rushmore National Memorial every year. They go rock climbing, hiking, and learn about the history of the Black Hills.

Pit Stop

Mount Rushmore is located near Rapid City, South Dakota—and so is Dinosaur Park! You can see life-size, concrete dinosaurs overlooking the Black Hills there.

Weird and Wonderful Pit Stops
in the
Midwest

World's Largest Muskie
Found at the National Freshwater Fishing Hall of Fame in Hayward, Wisconsin, this huge fish sculpture is as big as an airplane.

Carhenge
This sculpture, found in Alliance, Nebraska, is made of cars! It's modeled after Stonehenge, the ancient stone circle in England.

World's Largest Ketchup Bottle
What do you put on your burger? In Collinsville, Illinois, you'll really want to layer on the famous tomato spread after seeing this huge landmark!

Dorothy's House and Land of Oz
Follow the yellow brick road to Liberal, Kansas, to see the "real" house of Dorothy Gale from *The Wizard of Oz*.

World's Largest Ball of Twine
Every year visitors to Cawker City, Kansas, can go to a "twine-a-thon," during which residents of the town add to this mass of string.

Glossary

arch: a structure built in the shape of a curve

chili: a hearty soup commonly made with meat and beans

climate: the average weather conditions of a place over a period of time

descendant: a person who comes after another in a family

export: a good that is sold to another country

Louisiana Purchase: the area between the Mississippi River and the Rocky Mountains that the US government bought from France in 1803

mesa: a flat, raised area with steep sides

Northwest Territory: land east of the Mississippi River that the US government gained after the American Revolution. It became Ohio, Michigan, Indiana, Illinois, Wisconsin, and a small part of Minnesota.

region: an area

sacred: specially blessed

For More Information

Books

Johnson, Robin. *What's in the Midwest?* New York, NY: Crabtree Publishing, 2012.

Rau, Dana Meachen. *The Midwest.* New York, NY: Children's Press, 2012.

Websites

Chicago For Kids!
www.chicagoforkids.org
Use this site to explore the third-biggest US city.

Mount Rushmore
www.nps.gov/moru/index.htm
Check out lots of information and pictures of this national memorial.

States and Regions
www.harcourtschool.com/ss1/adventure_activities/grade4.html
Use this interactive website to learn more about the regions of the United States.

Index